Color by Number Adult Coloring Book

This Color by Number Book belongs to:

_____

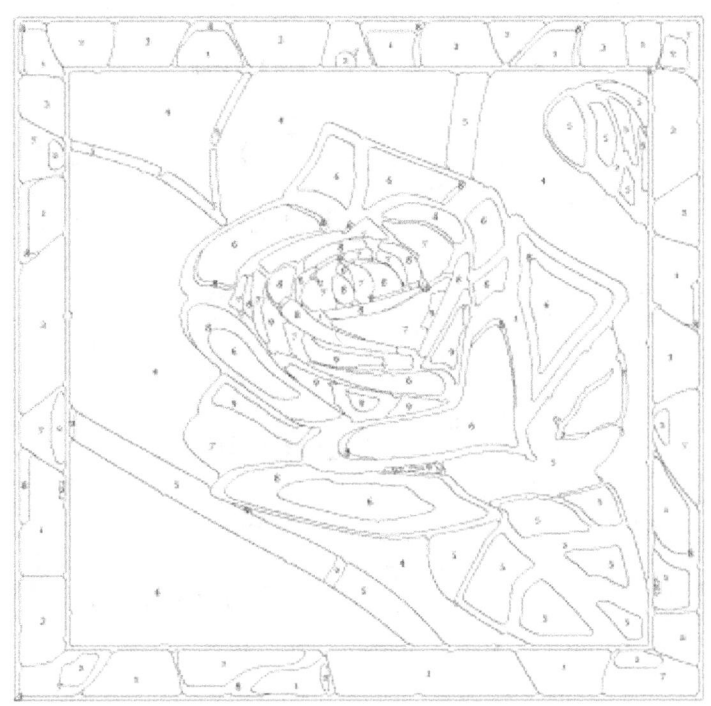

Copyright © 2020 Adult Puzzle Books

1. Black
2. Blue
3. Light Blue
4. Brown
5. Dark Red
6. Orange
7. Yellow
8. Purple
9. Pink
10. Gold
11. Green
12. Gold
13. Red
14. Dark Green

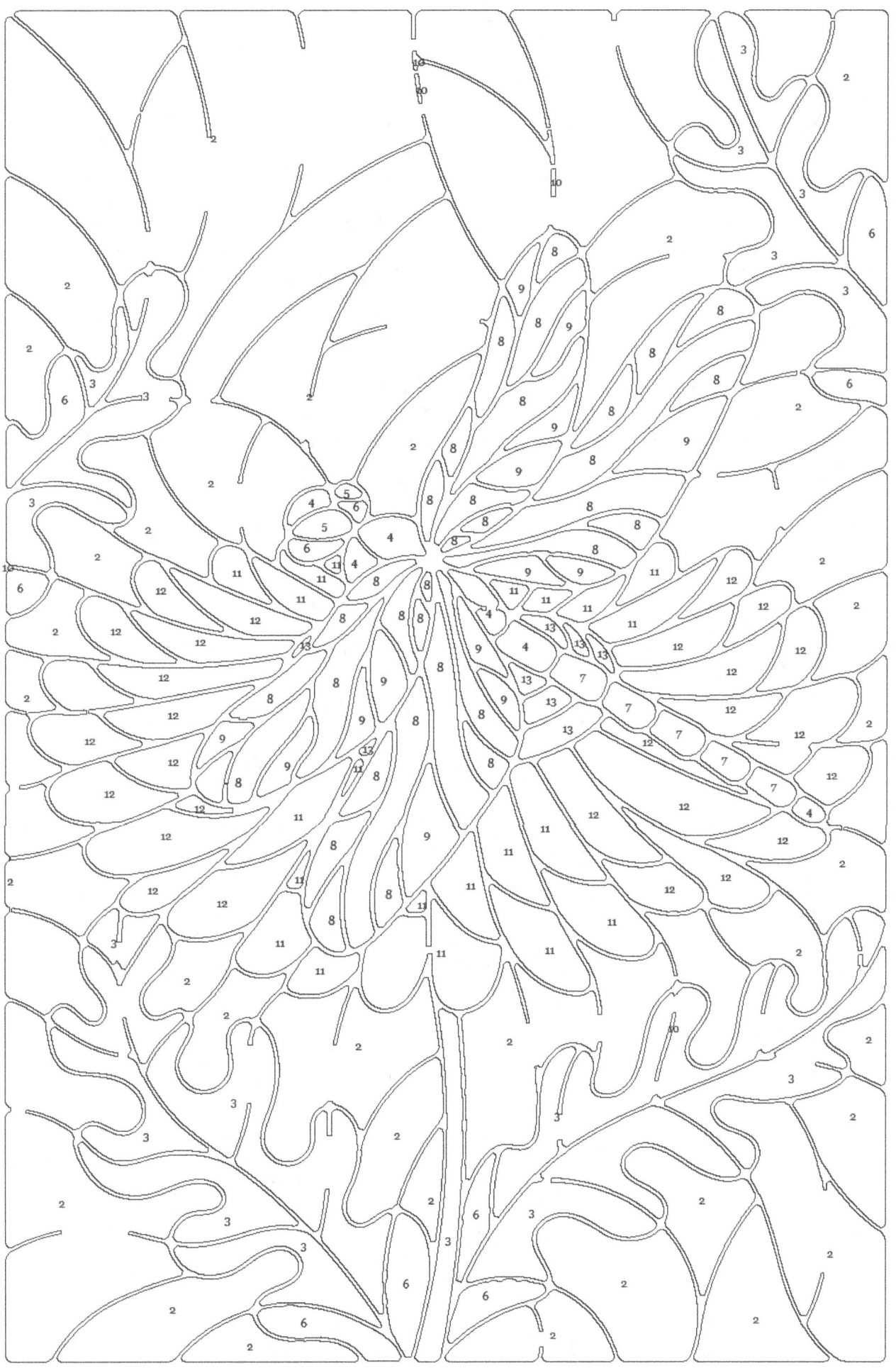

1. Black
2. Blue
3. Light Blue
4. Brown
5. Dark Red
6. Orange
7. Yellow
8. Purple
9. Pink
10. Gold
11. Green
12. Gold
13. Red
14. Dark Green

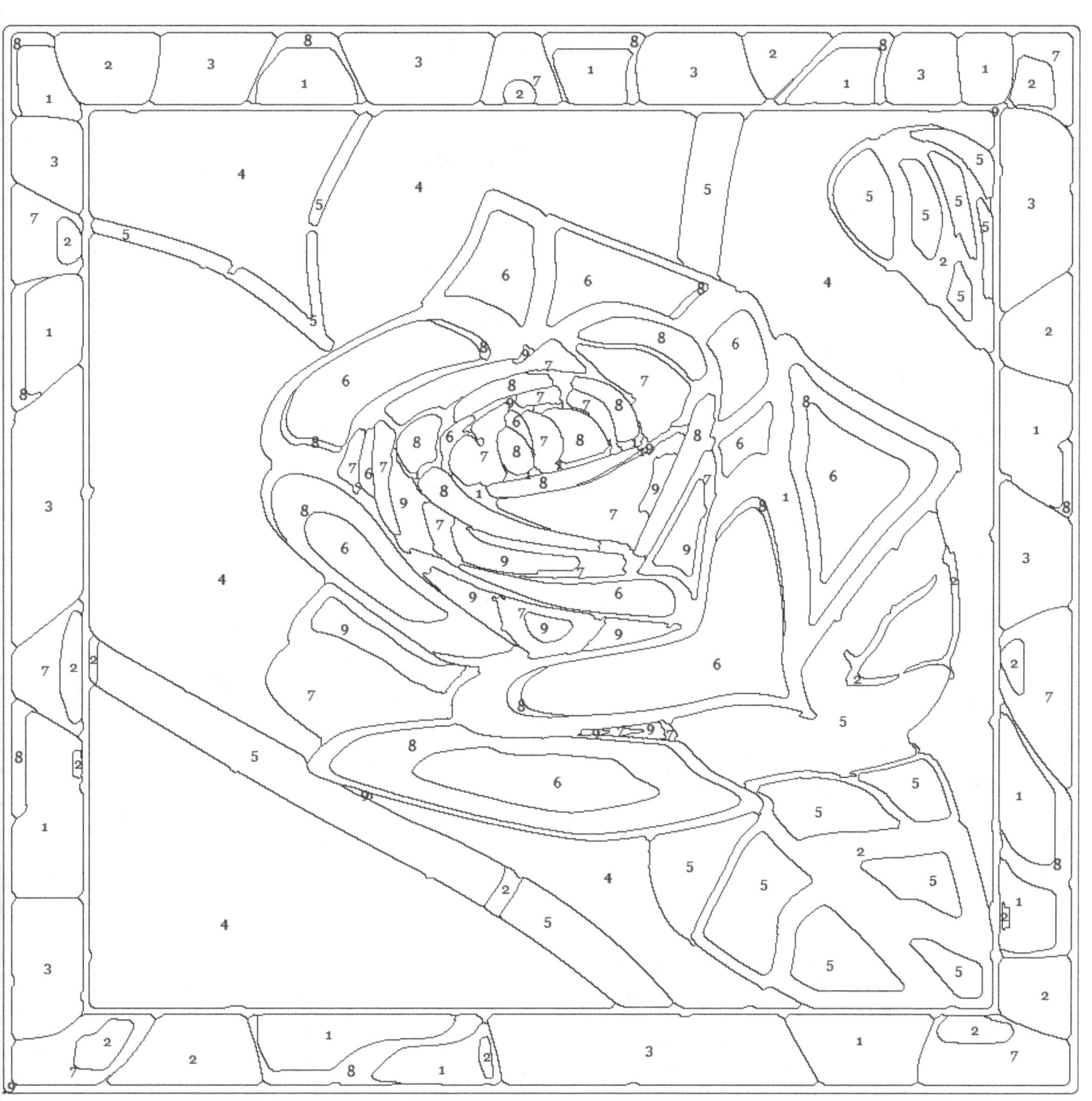

1. Black
2. Blue
3. Light Blue
4. Brown
5. Dark Red
6. Orange
7. Yellow
8. Purple
9. Pink
10. Gold
11. Green
12. Gold
13. Red
14. Dark Green

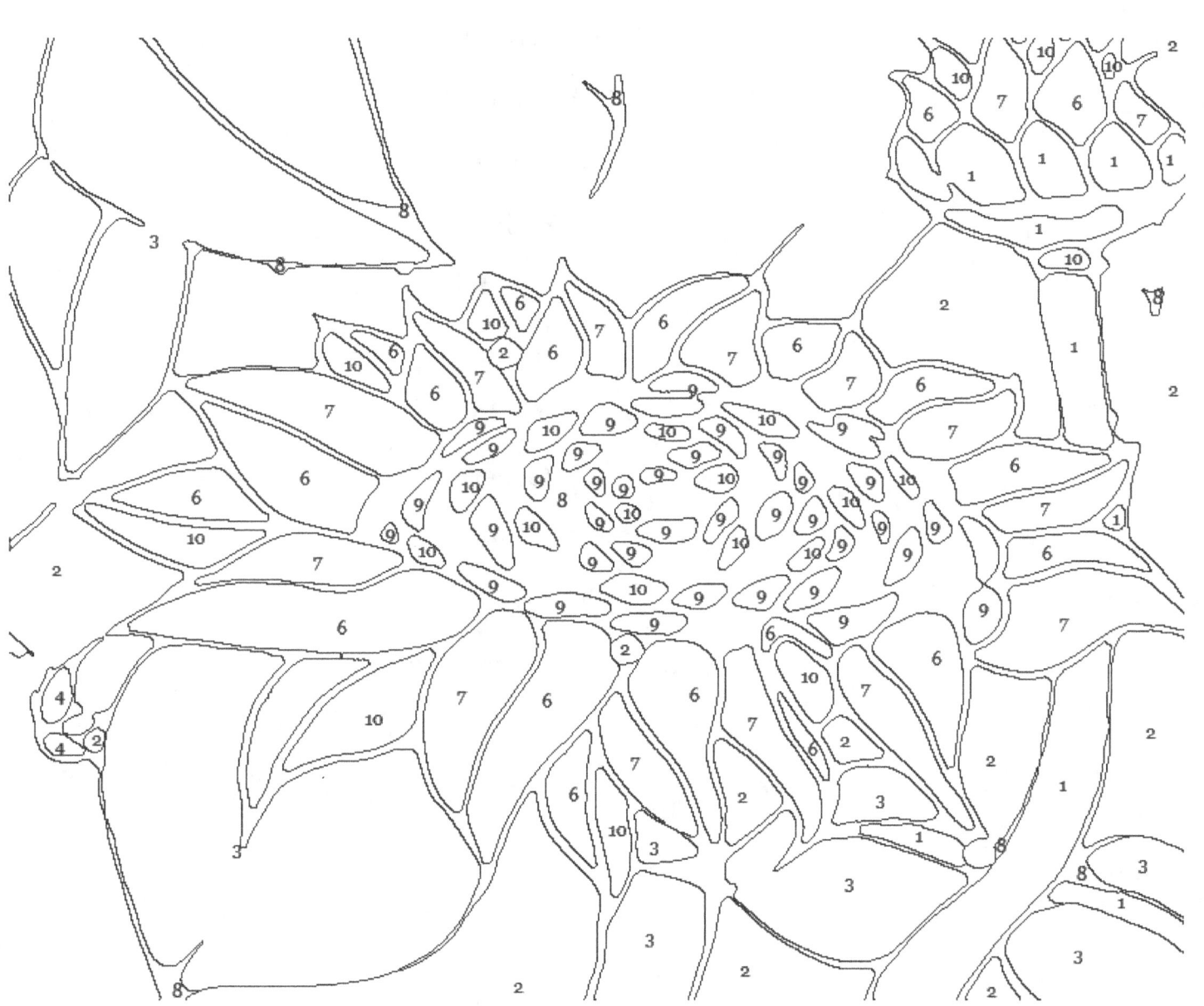

1. Black
2. Blue
3. Light Blue
4. Brown
5. Dark Red
6. Orange
7. Yellow
8. Purple
9. Pink
10. Gold
11. Green
12. Gold
13. Red
14. Dark Green

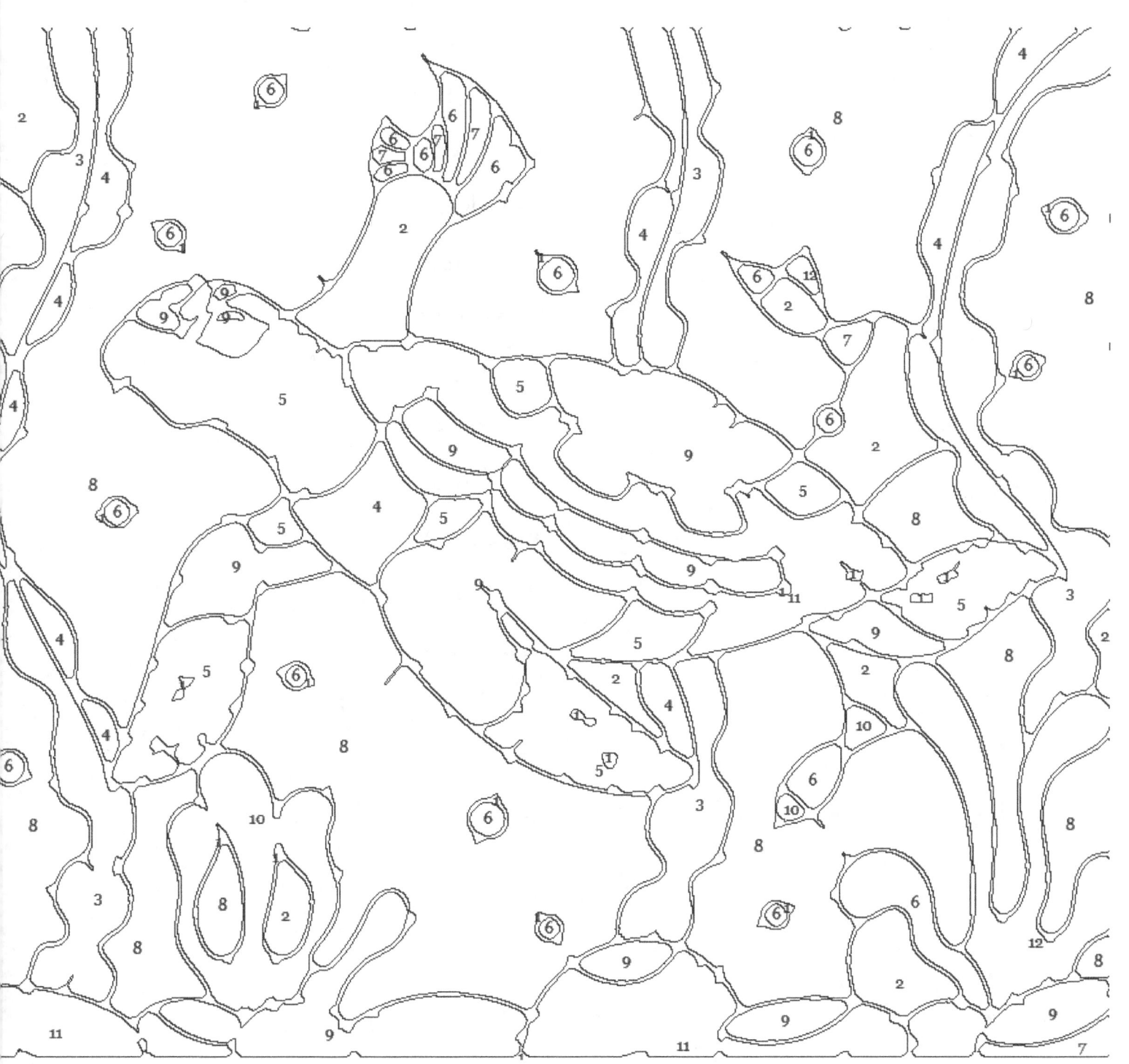

1. Black
2. Blue
3. Light Blue
4. Brown
5. Dark Red
6. Orange
7. Yellow
8. Purple
9. Pink
10. Gold
11. Green
12. Gold
13. Red
14. Dark Green

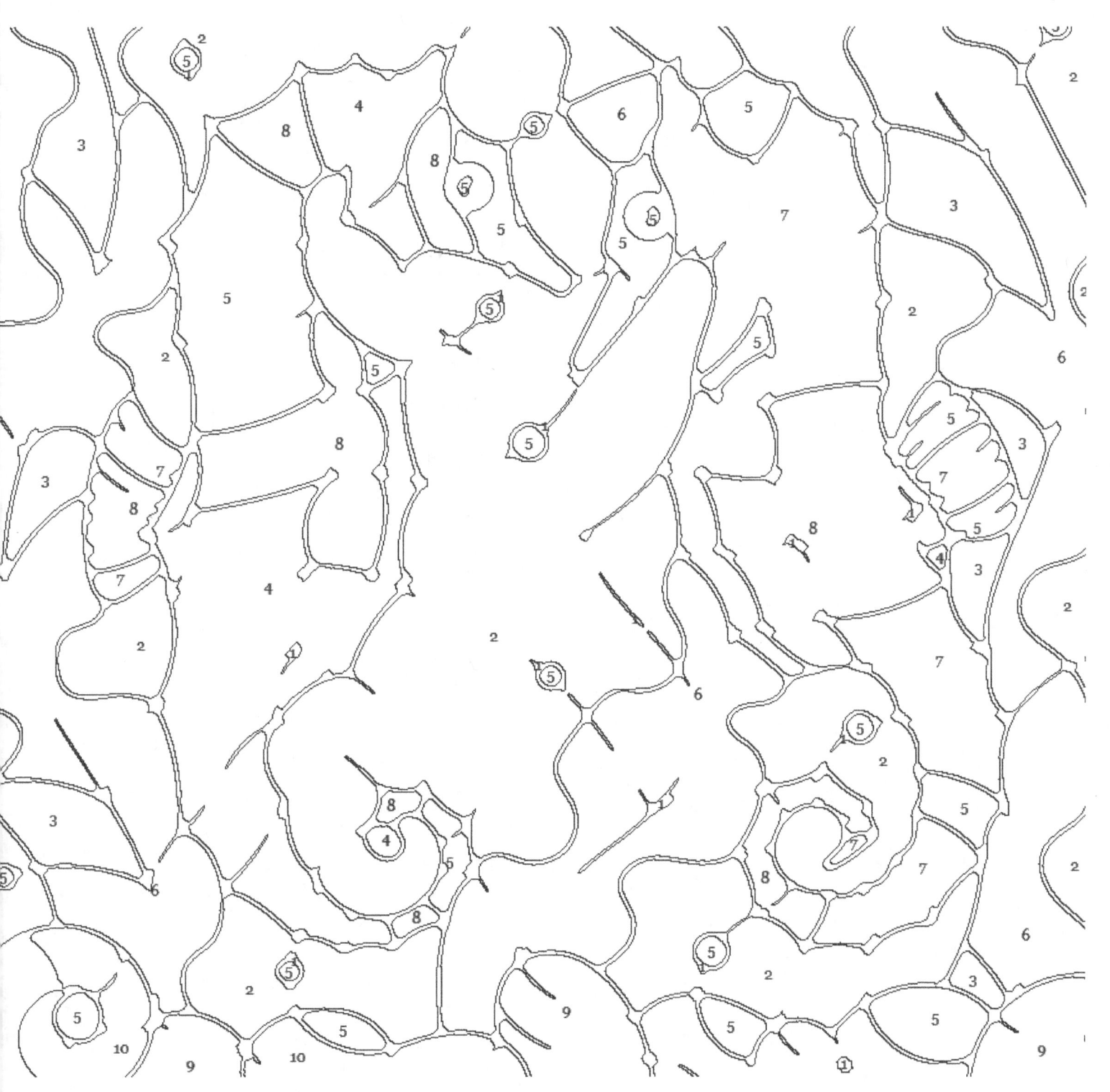

1. Black
2. Blue
3. Light Blue
4. Brown
5. Dark Red
6. Orange
7. Yellow
8. Purple
9. Pink
10. Gold
11. Green
12. Gold
13. Red
14. Dark Green

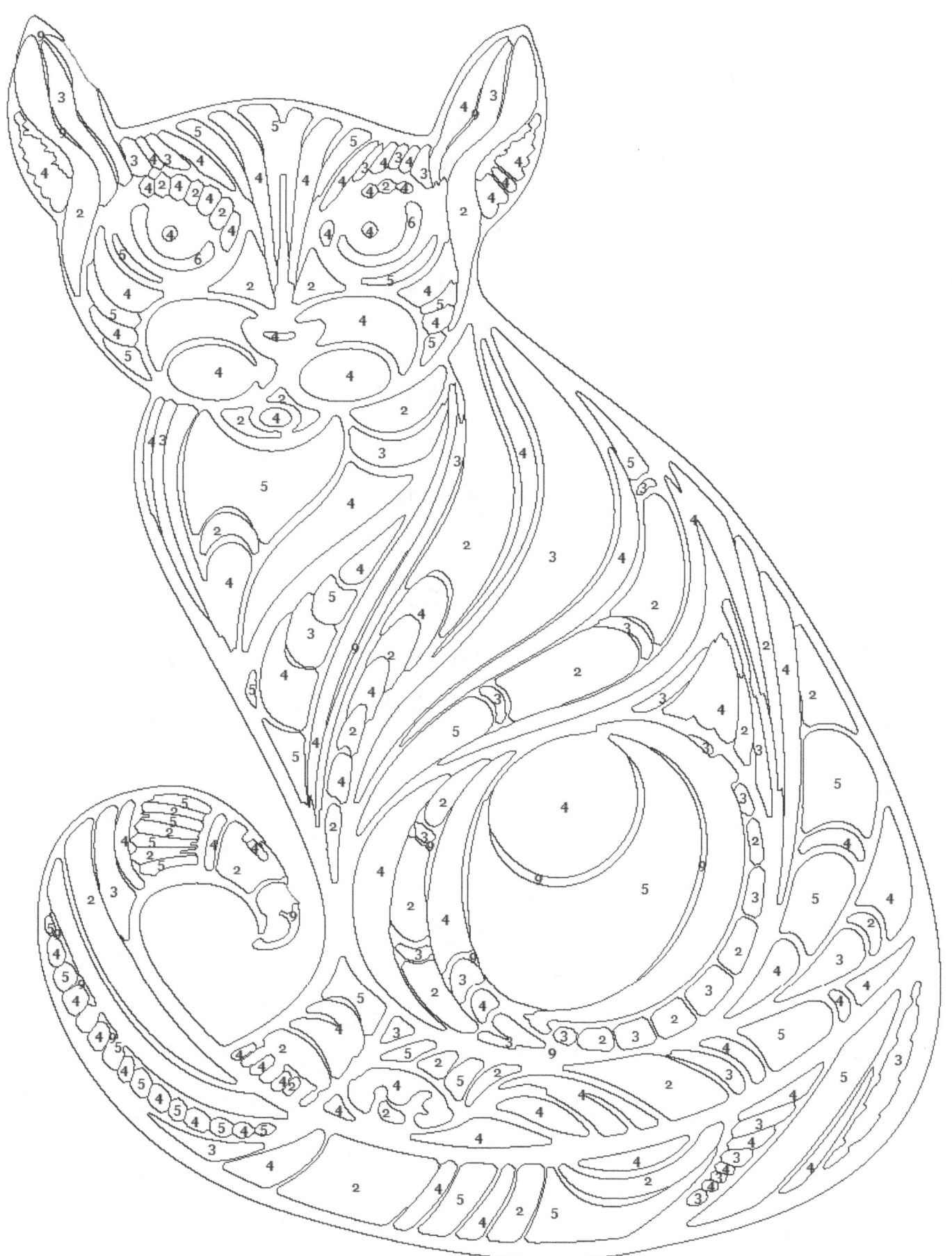

1. Black
2. Blue
3. Light Blue
4. Brown
5. Dark Red
6. Orange
7. Yellow
8. Purple
9. Pink
10. Gold
11. Green
12. Gold
13. Red
14. Dark Green

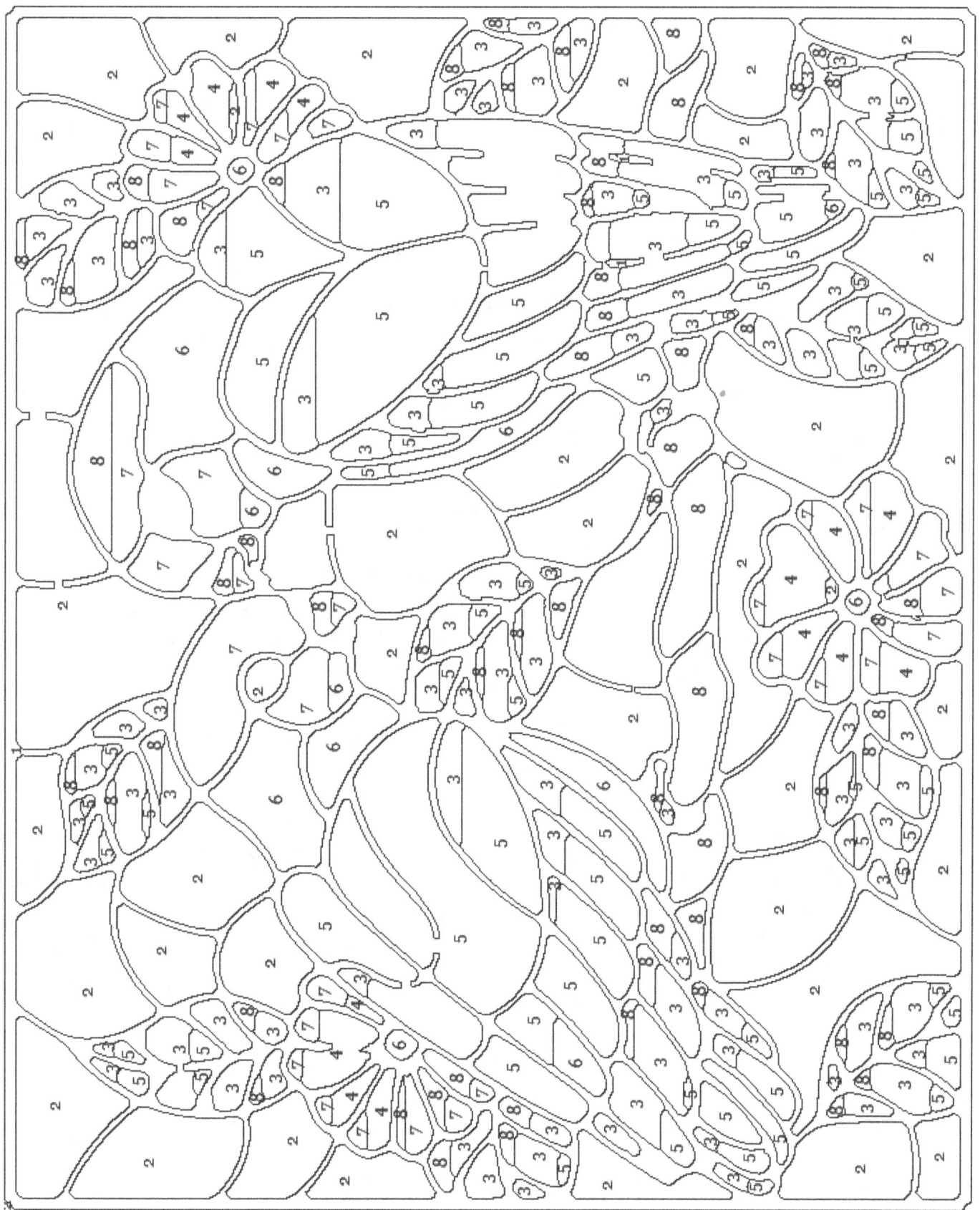

1. Black
2. Blue
3. Light Blue
4. Brown
5. Dark Red
6. Orange
7. Yellow
8. Purple
9. Pink
10. Gold
11. Green
12. Gold
13. Red
14. Dark Green

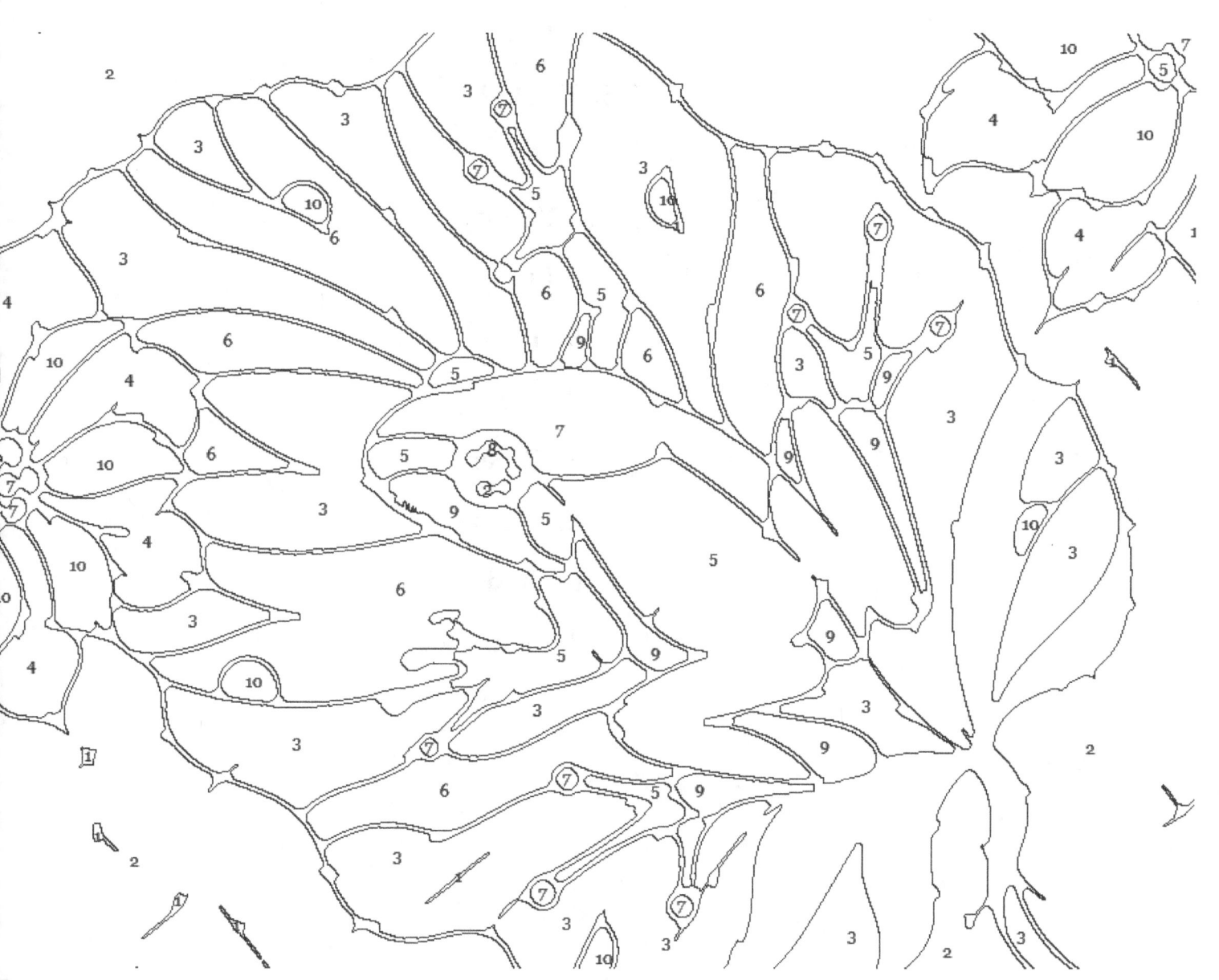

1. Black
2. Blue
3. Light Blue
4. Brown
5. Dark Red
6. Orange
7. Yellow
8. Purple
9. Pink
10. Gold
11. Green
12. Gold
13. Red
14. Dark Green

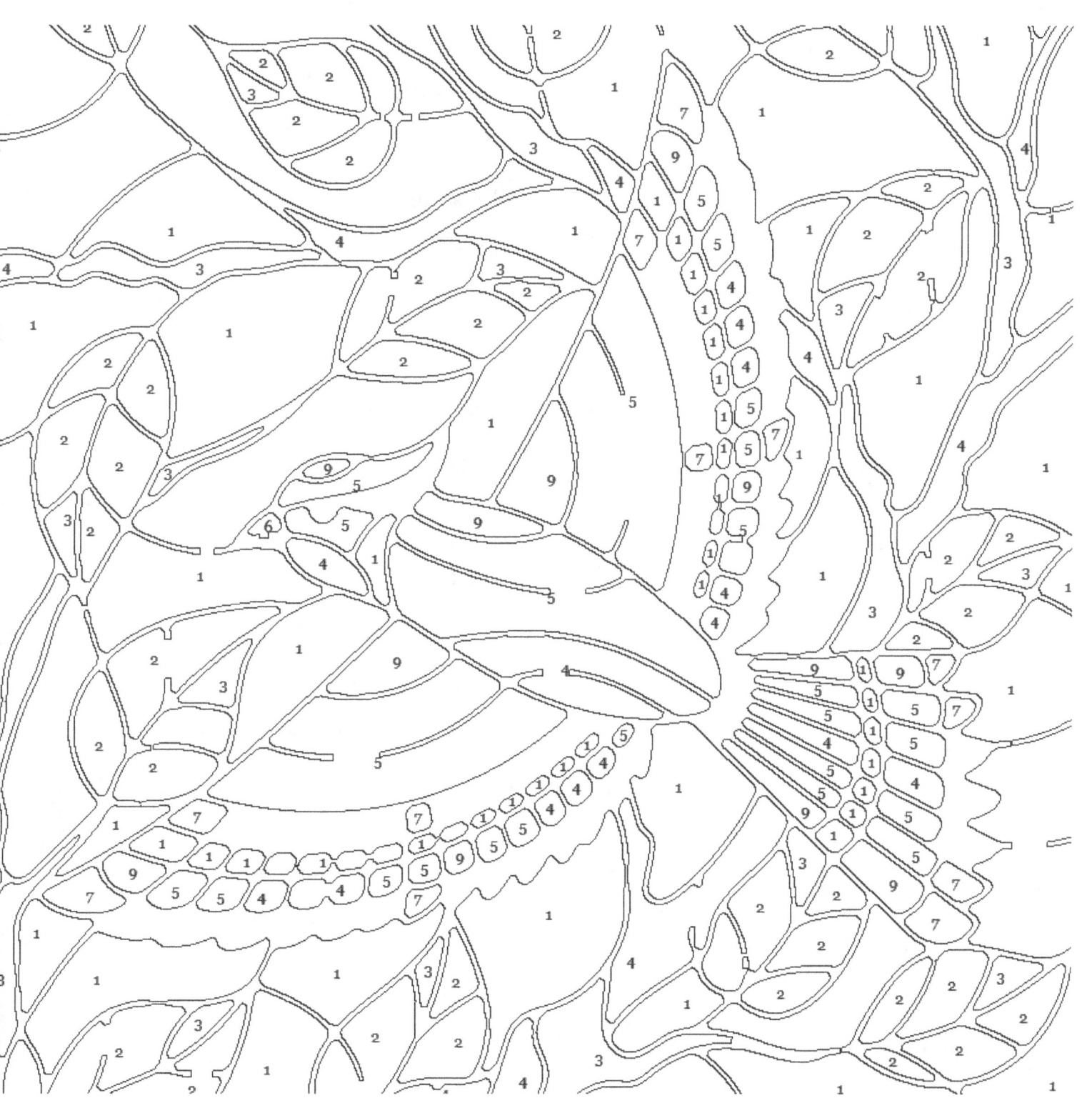

1. Black
2. Blue
3. Light Blue
4. Brown
5. Dark Red
6. Orange
7. Yellow
8. Purple
9. Pink
10. Gold
11. Green
12. Gold
13. Red
14. Dark Green

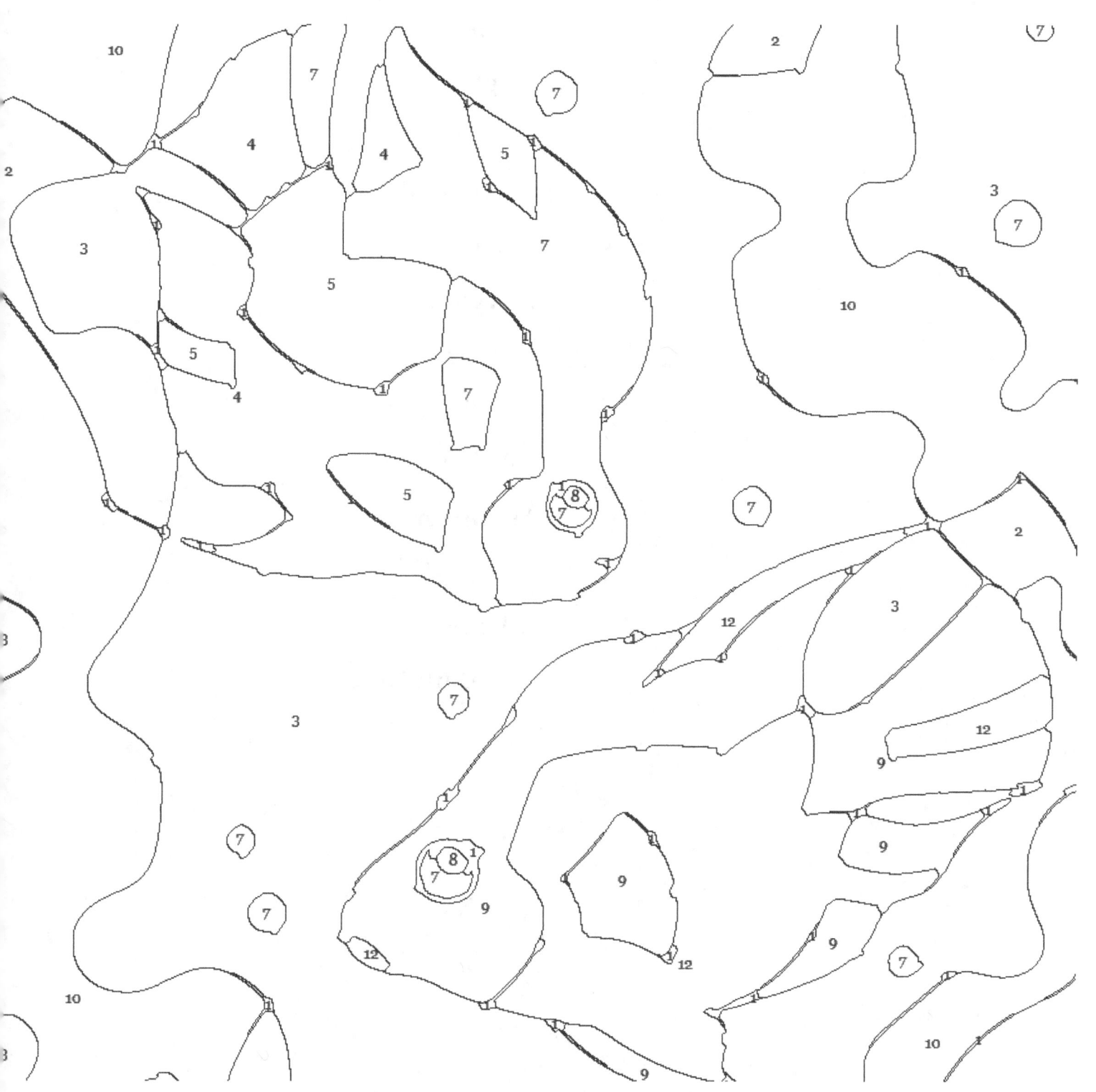

1. Black
2. Blue
3. Light Blue
4. Brown
5. Dark Red
6. Orange
7. Yellow
8. Purple
9. Pink
10. Gold
11. Green
12. Gold
13. Red
14. Dark Green

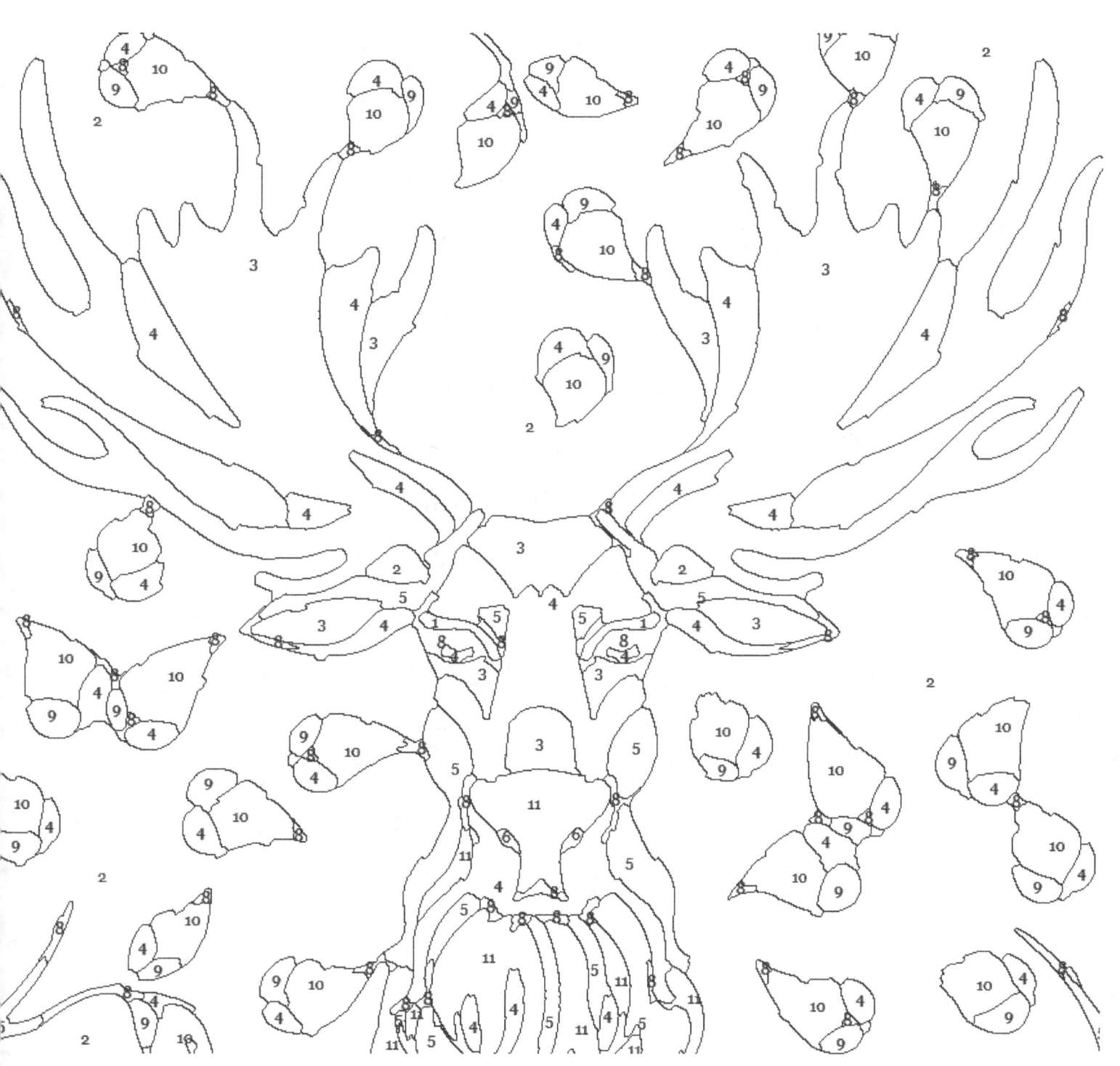

1. Black
2. Blue
3. Light Blue
4. Brown
5. Dark Red
6. Orange
7. Yellow
8. Purple
9. Pink
10. Gold
11. Green
12. Gold
13. Red
14. Dark Green

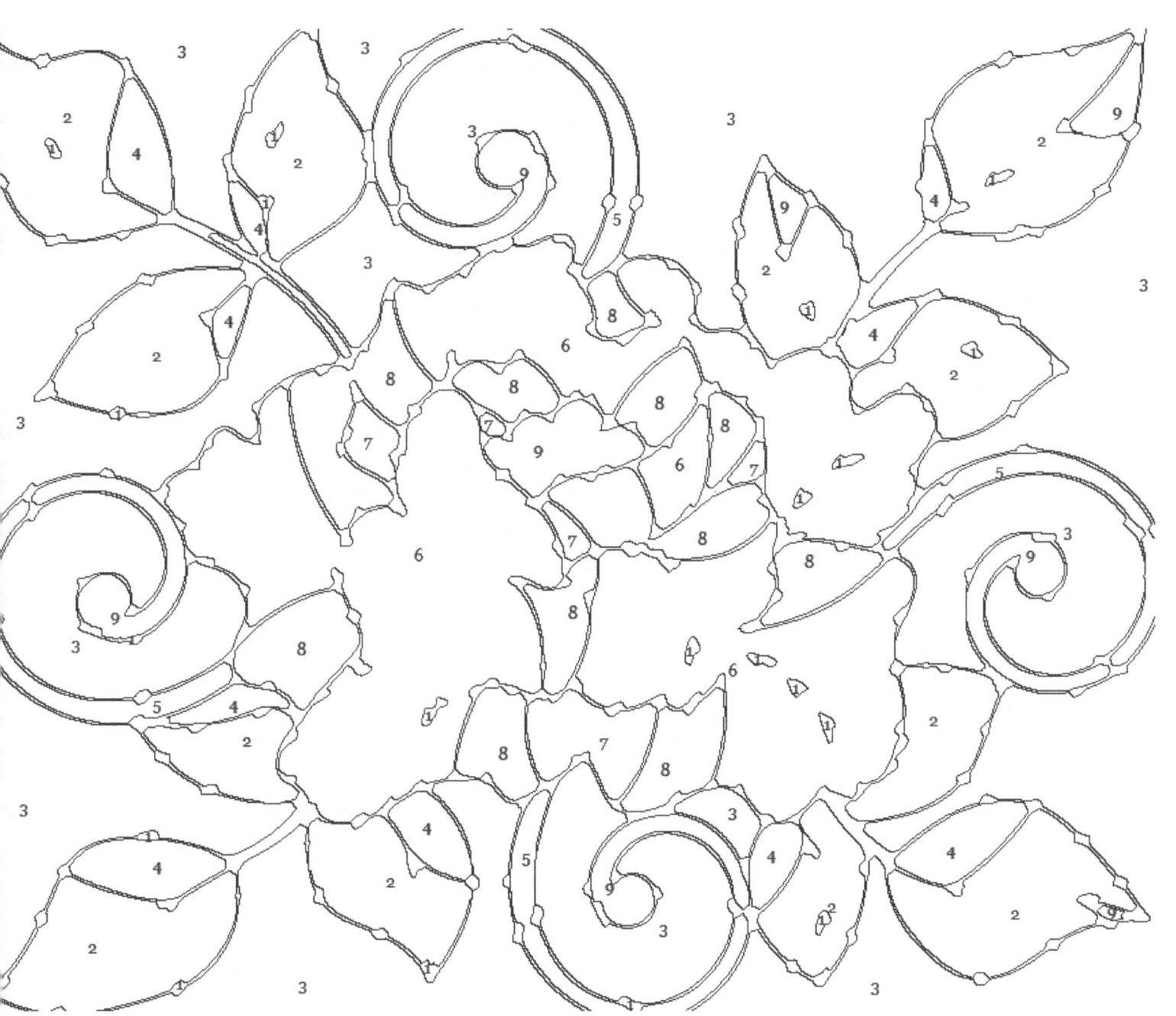

1. Black
2. Blue
3. Light Blue
4. Brown
5. Dark Red
6. Orange
7. Yellow
8. Purple
9. Pink
10. Gold
11. Green
12. Gold
13. Red
14. Dark Green

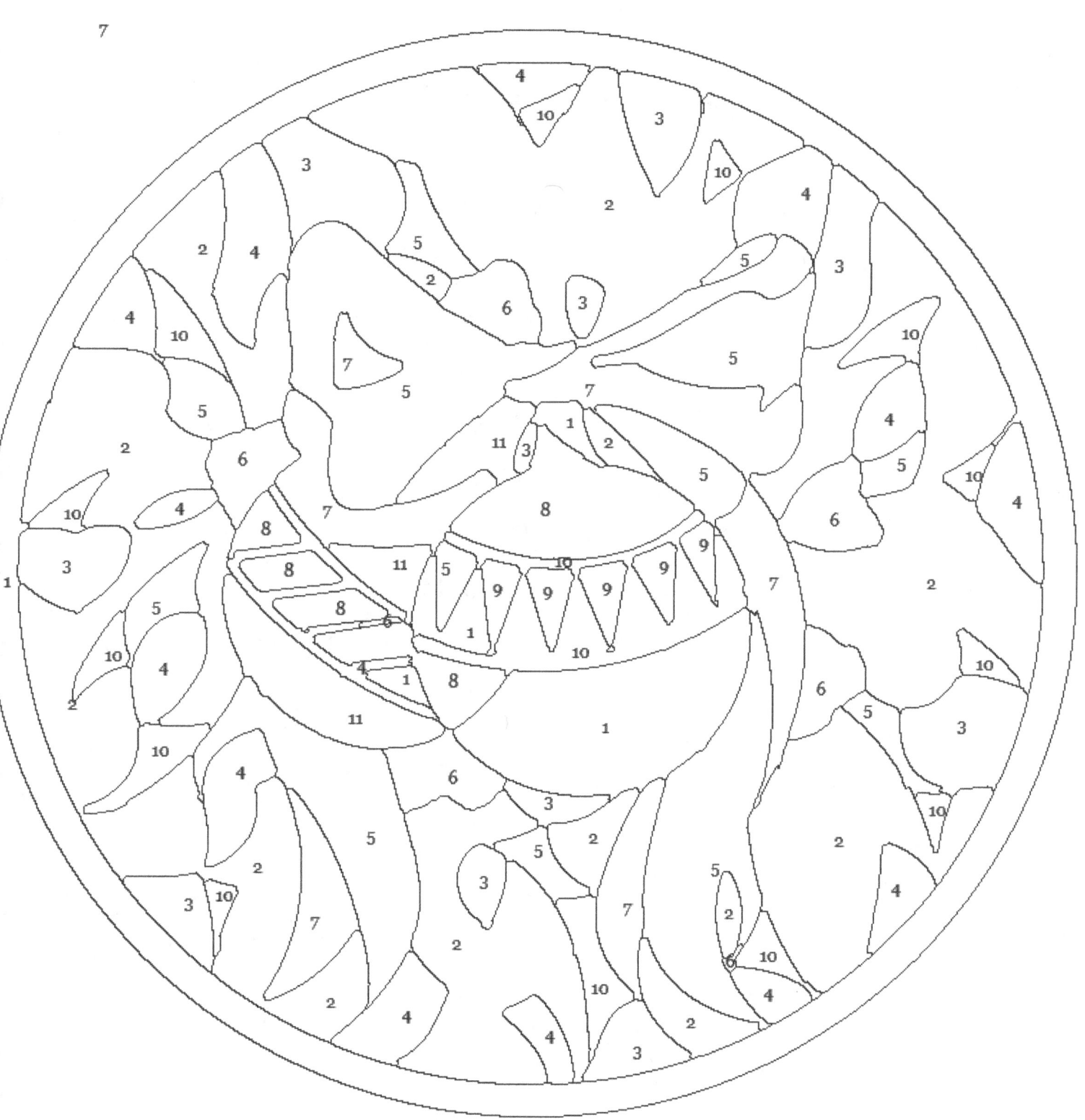

1. Black
2. Blue
3. Light Blue
4. Brown
5. Dark Red
6. Orange
7. Yellow
8. Purple
9. Pink
10. Gold
11. Green
12. Gold
13. Red
14. Dark Green

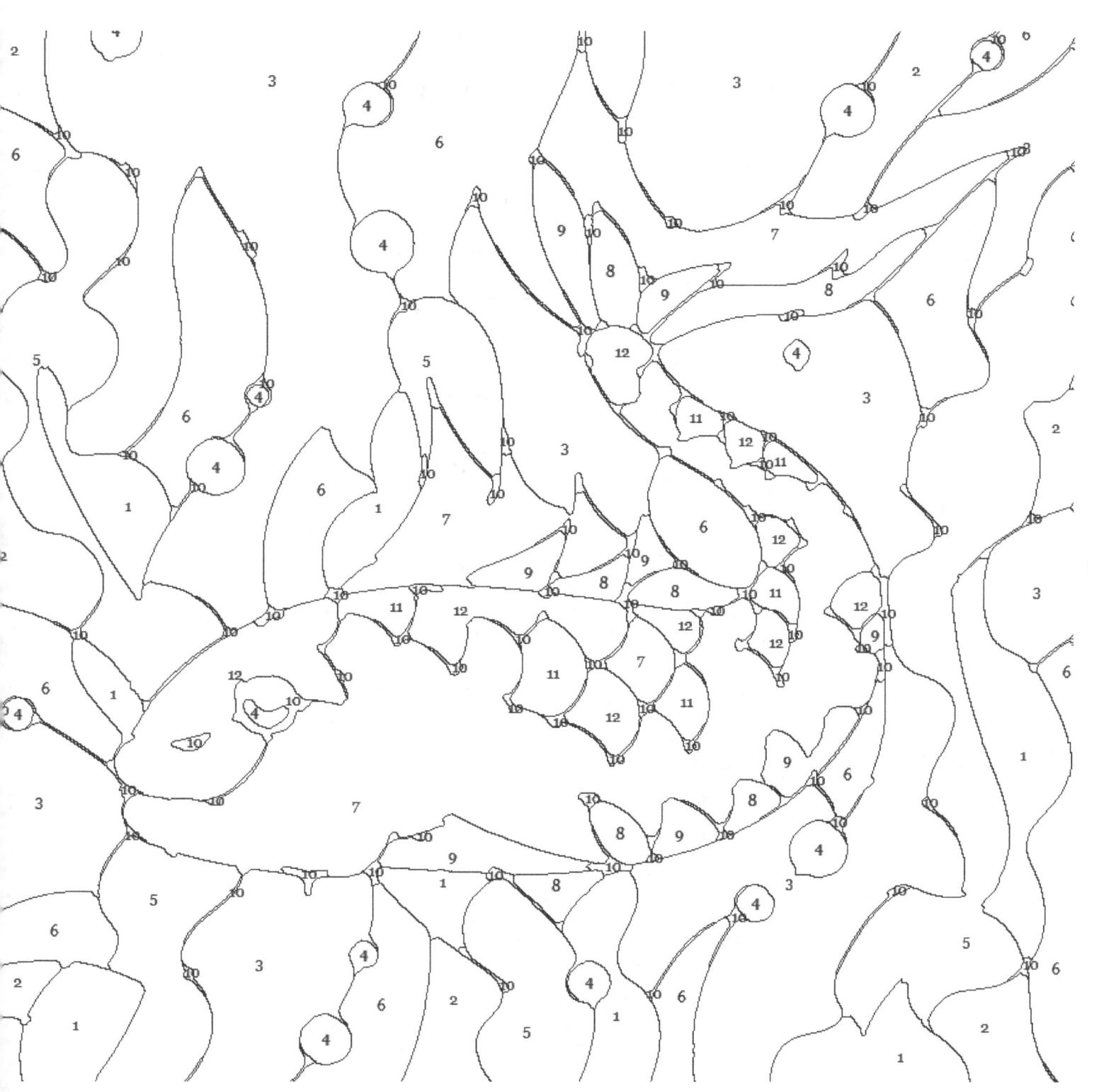

1. Black
2. Blue
3. Light Blue
4. Brown
5. Dark Red
6. Orange
7. Yellow
8. Purple
9. Pink
10. Gold
11. Green
12. Gold
13. Red
14. Dark Green

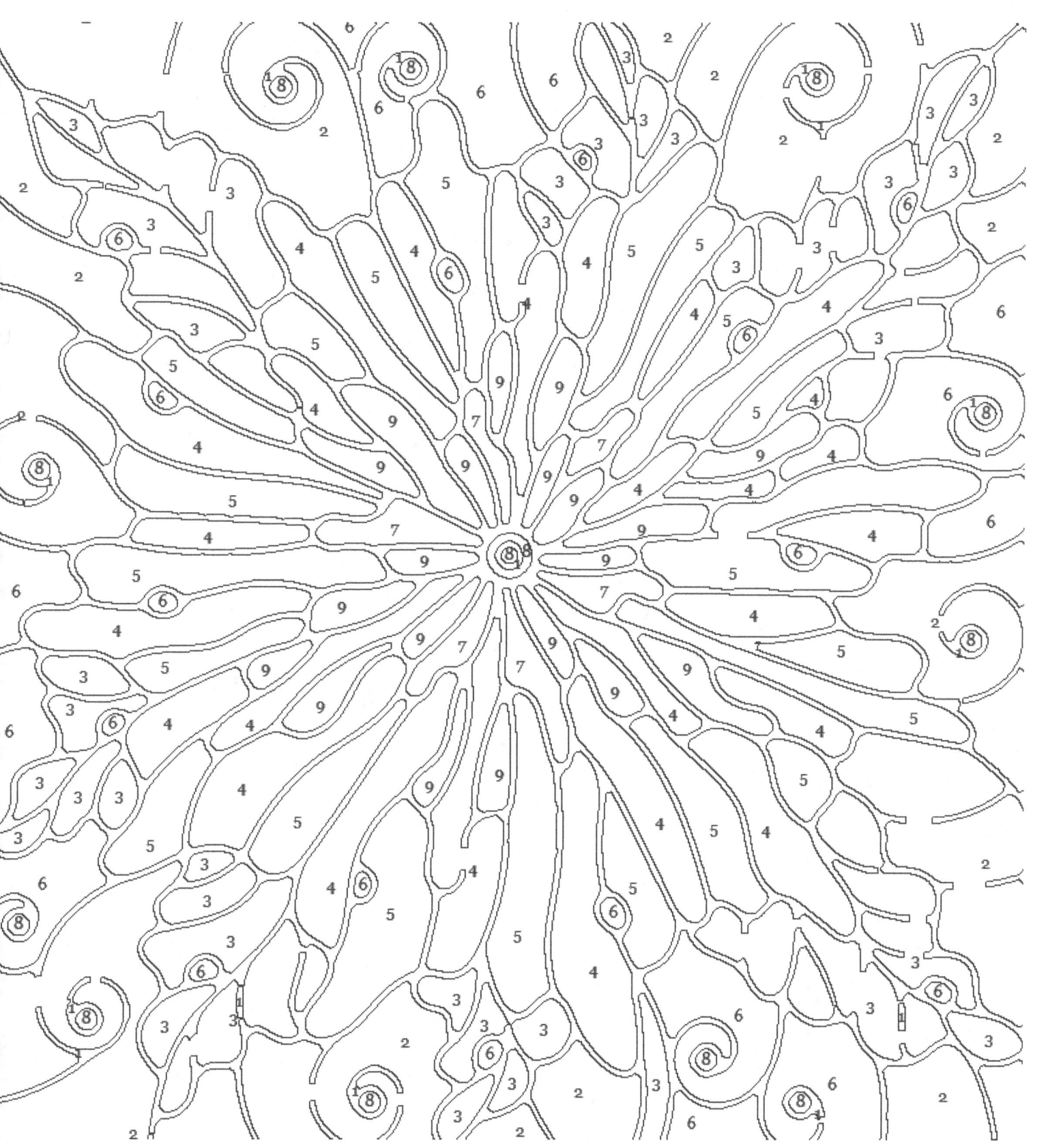

1. Black
2. Blue
3. Light Blue
4. Brown
5. Dark Red
6. Orange
7. Yellow
8. Purple
9. Pink
10. Gold
11. Green
12. Gold
13. Red
14. Dark Green

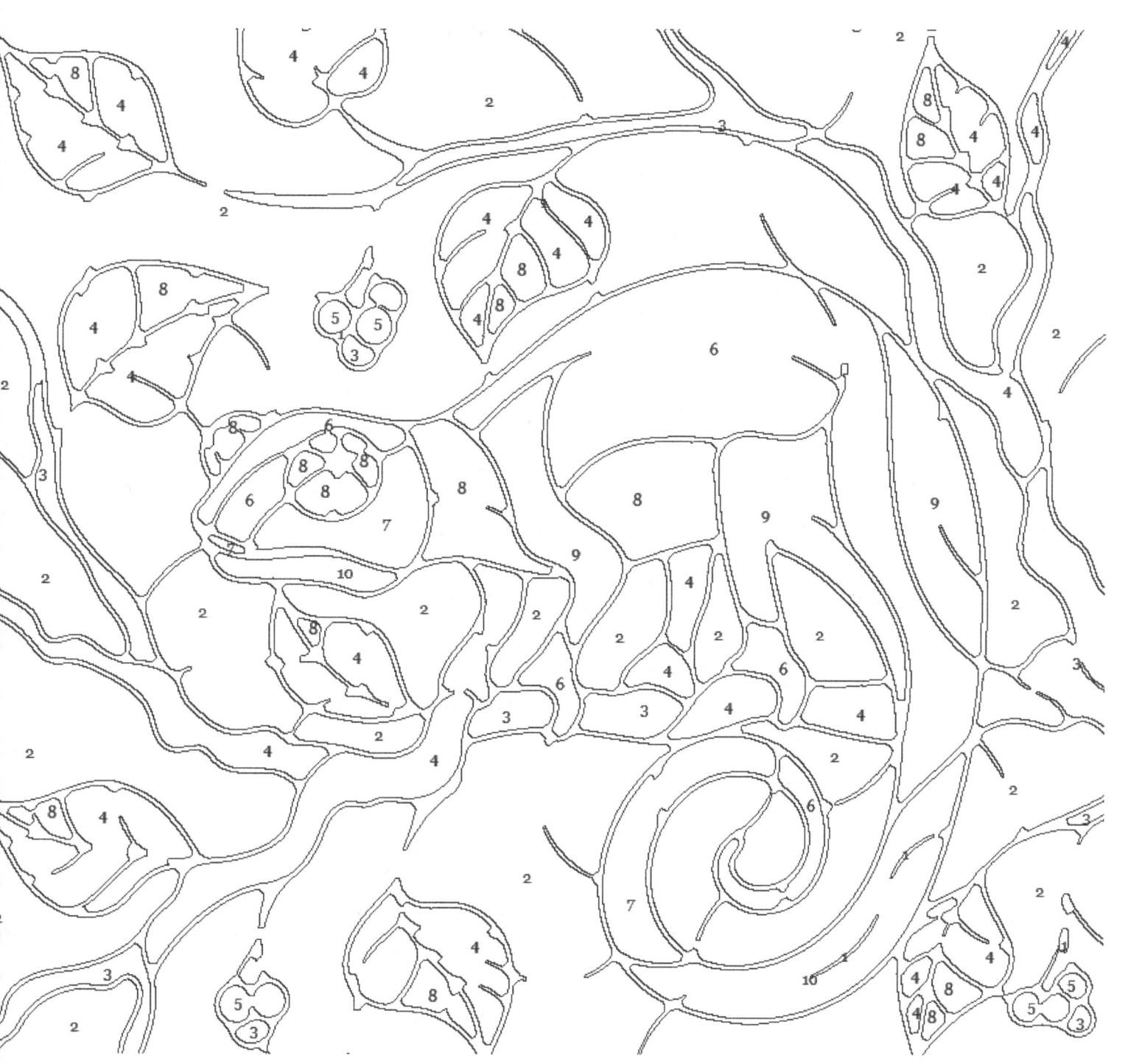

1. Black
2. Blue
3. Light Blue
4. Brown
5. Dark Red
6. Orange
7. Yellow
8. Purple
9. Pink
10. Gold
11. Green
12. Gold
13. Red
14. Dark Green

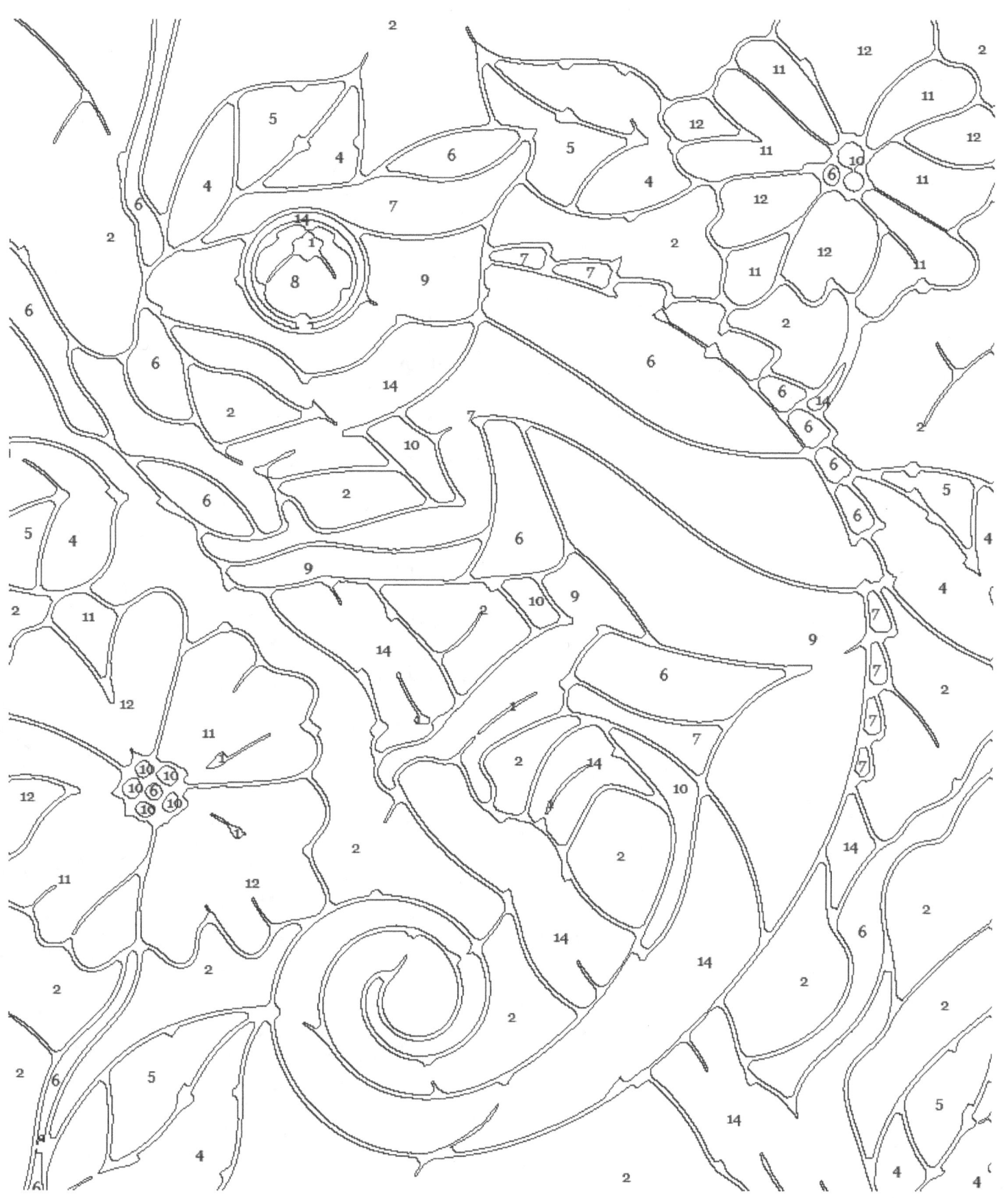

1. Black
2. Blue
3. Light Blue
4. Brown
5. Dark Red
6. Orange
7. Yellow
8. Purple
9. Pink
10. Gold
11. Green
12. Gold
13. Red
14. Dark Green

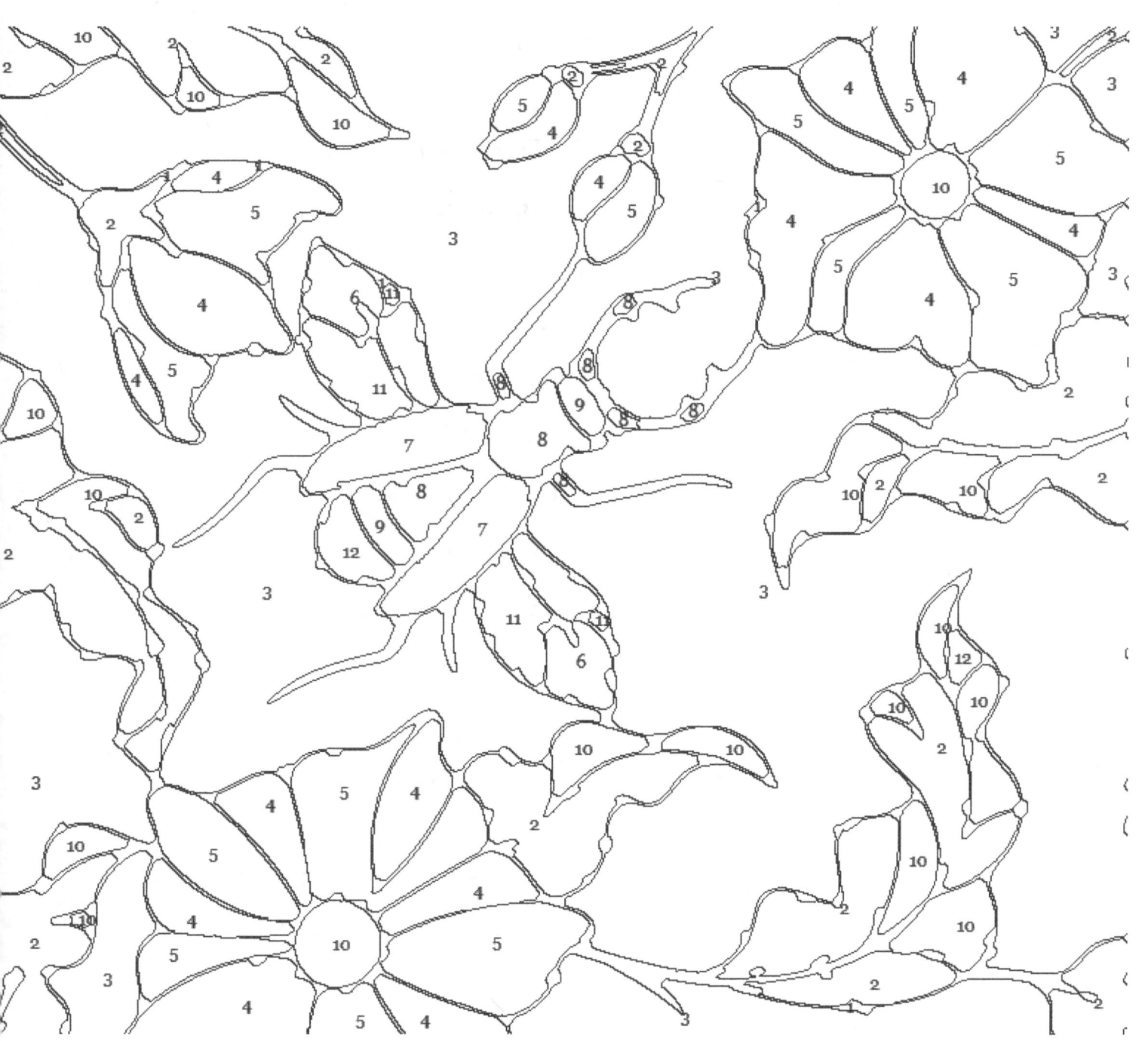

1. Black
2. Blue
3. Light Blue
4. Brown
5. Dark Red
6. Orange
7. Yellow
8. Purple
9. Pink
10. Gold
11. Green
12. Gold
13. Red
14. Dark Green

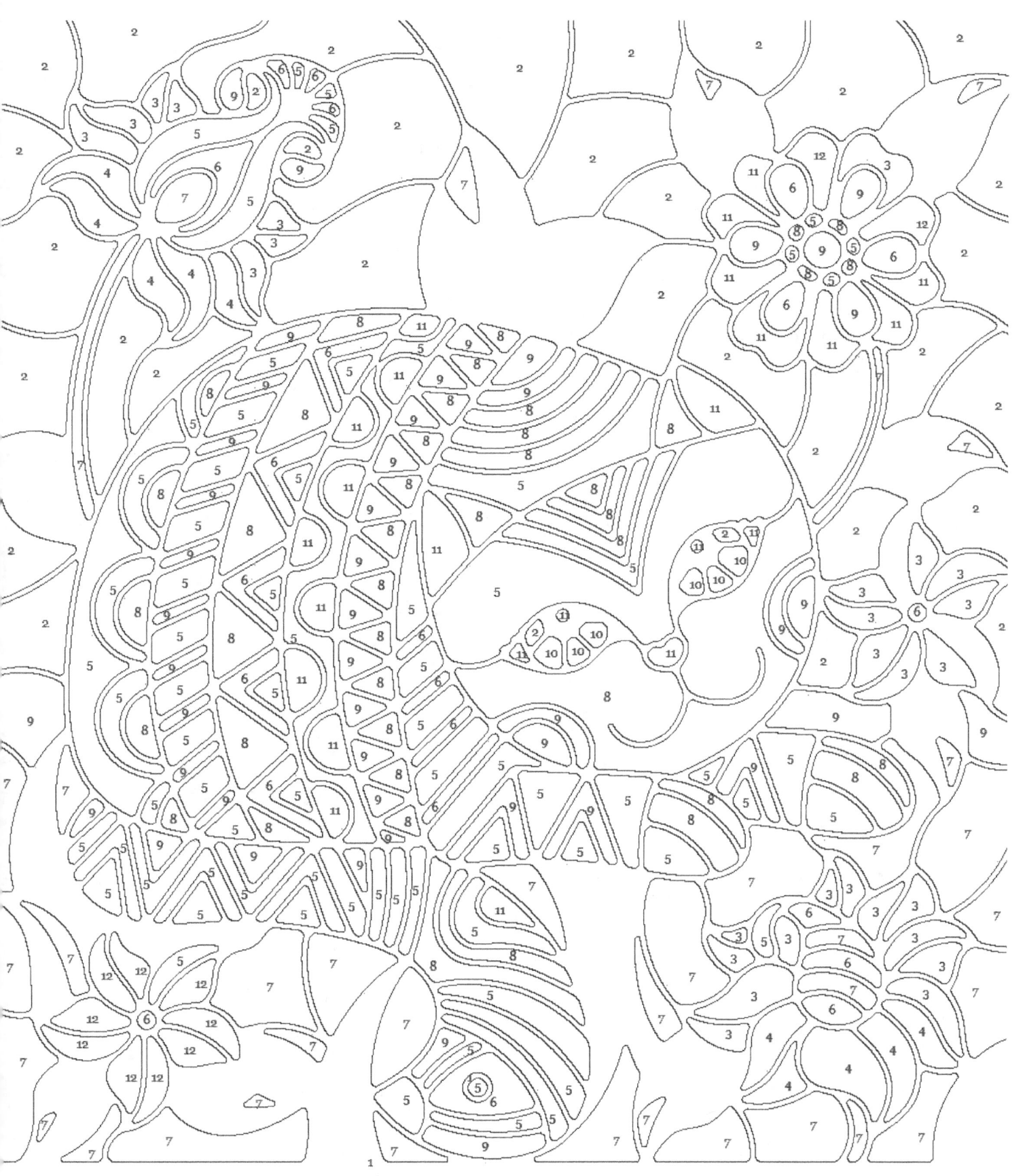

1. Black
2. Blue
3. Light Blue
4. Brown
5. Dark Red
6. Orange
7. Yellow
8. Purple
9. Pink
10. Gold
11. Green
12. Gold
13. Red
14. Dark Green

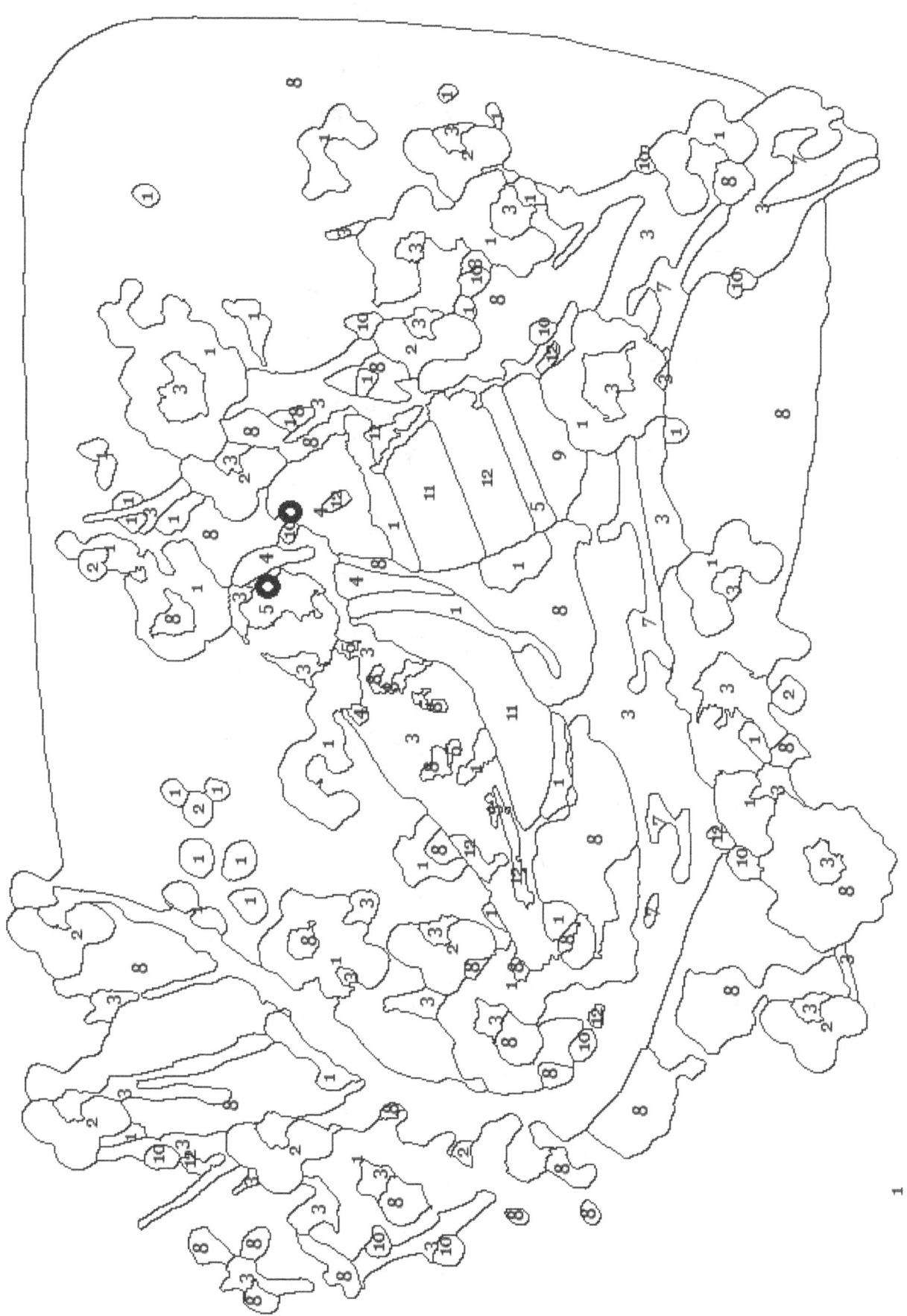

1. Black

2. Blue

3. Light Blue

4. Brown

5. Dark Red

6. Orange

7. Yellow

8. Purple

9. Pink

10. Gold

11. Green

12. Gold

13. Red

14. Dark Green

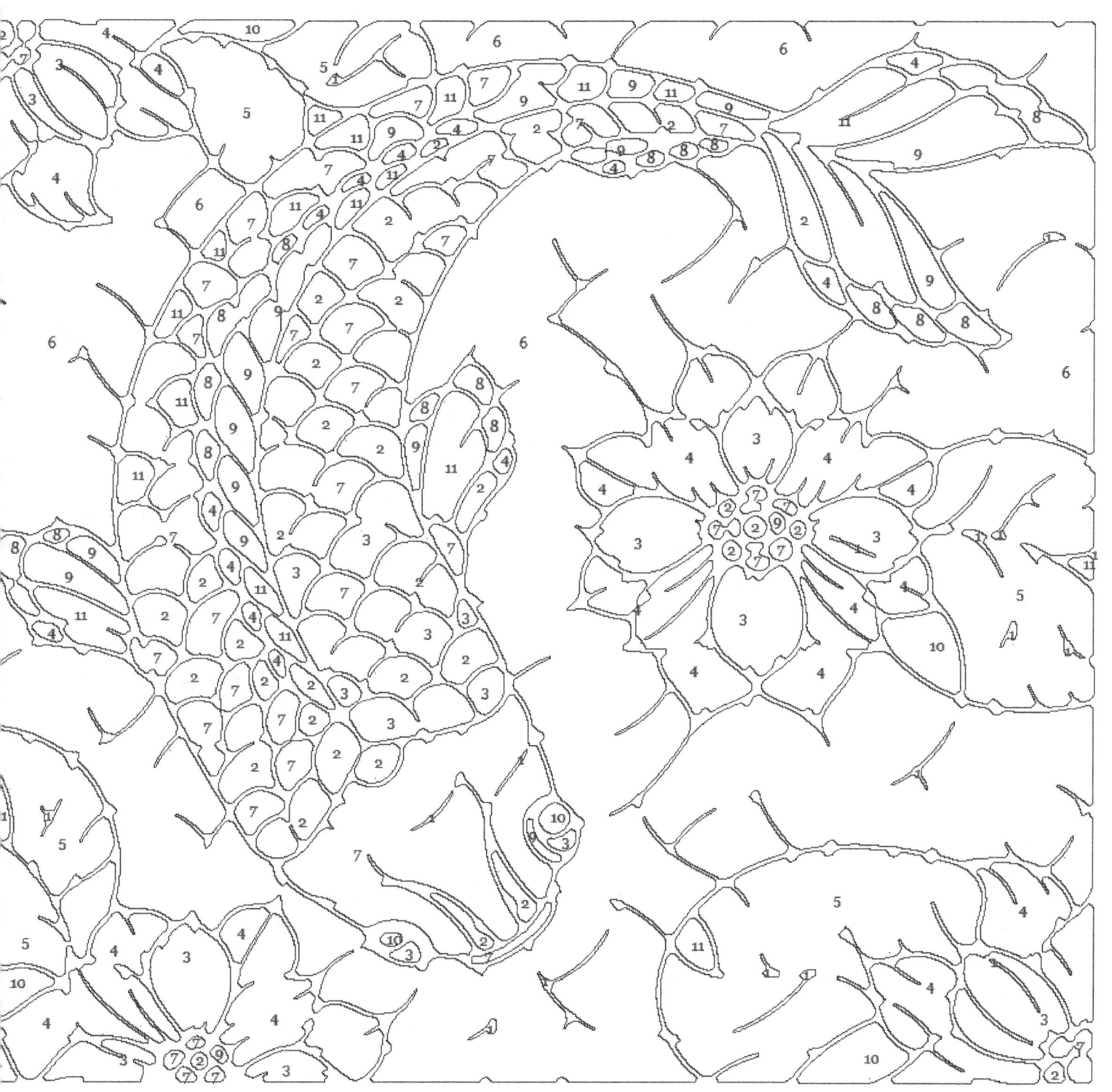

1. Black
2. Blue
3. Light Blue
4. Brown
5. Dark Red
6. Orange
7. Yellow
8. Purple
9. Pink
10. Gold
11. Green
12. Gold
13. Red
14. Dark Green

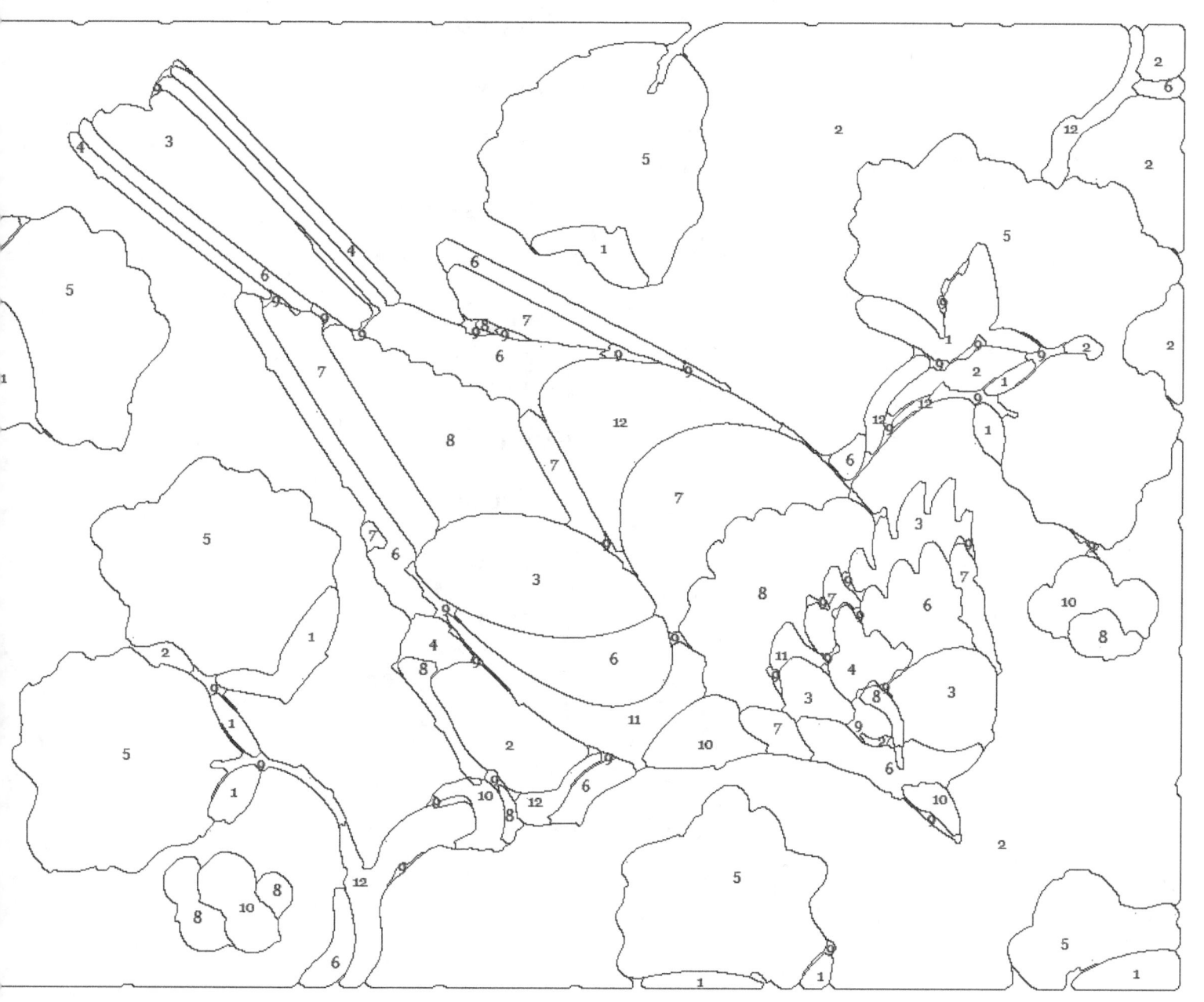

1. Black
2. Blue
3. Light Blue
4. Brown
5. Dark Red
6. Orange
7. Yellow
8. Purple
9. Pink
10. Gold
11. Green
12. Gold
13. Red
14. Dark Green

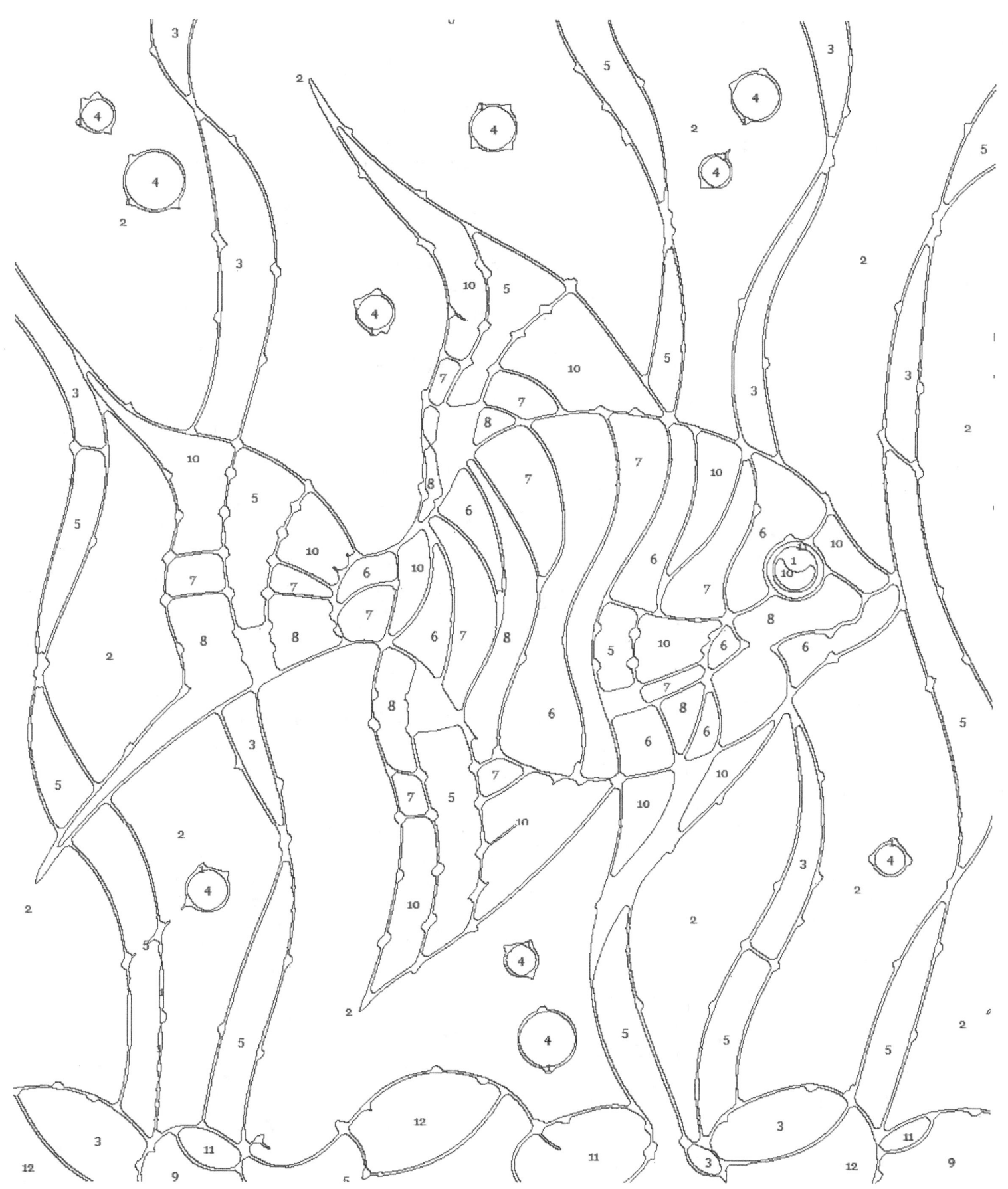

1. Black
2. Blue
3. Light Blue
4. Brown
5. Dark Red
6. Orange
7. Yellow
8. Purple
9. Pink
10. Gold
11. Green
12. Gold
13. Red
14. Dark Green

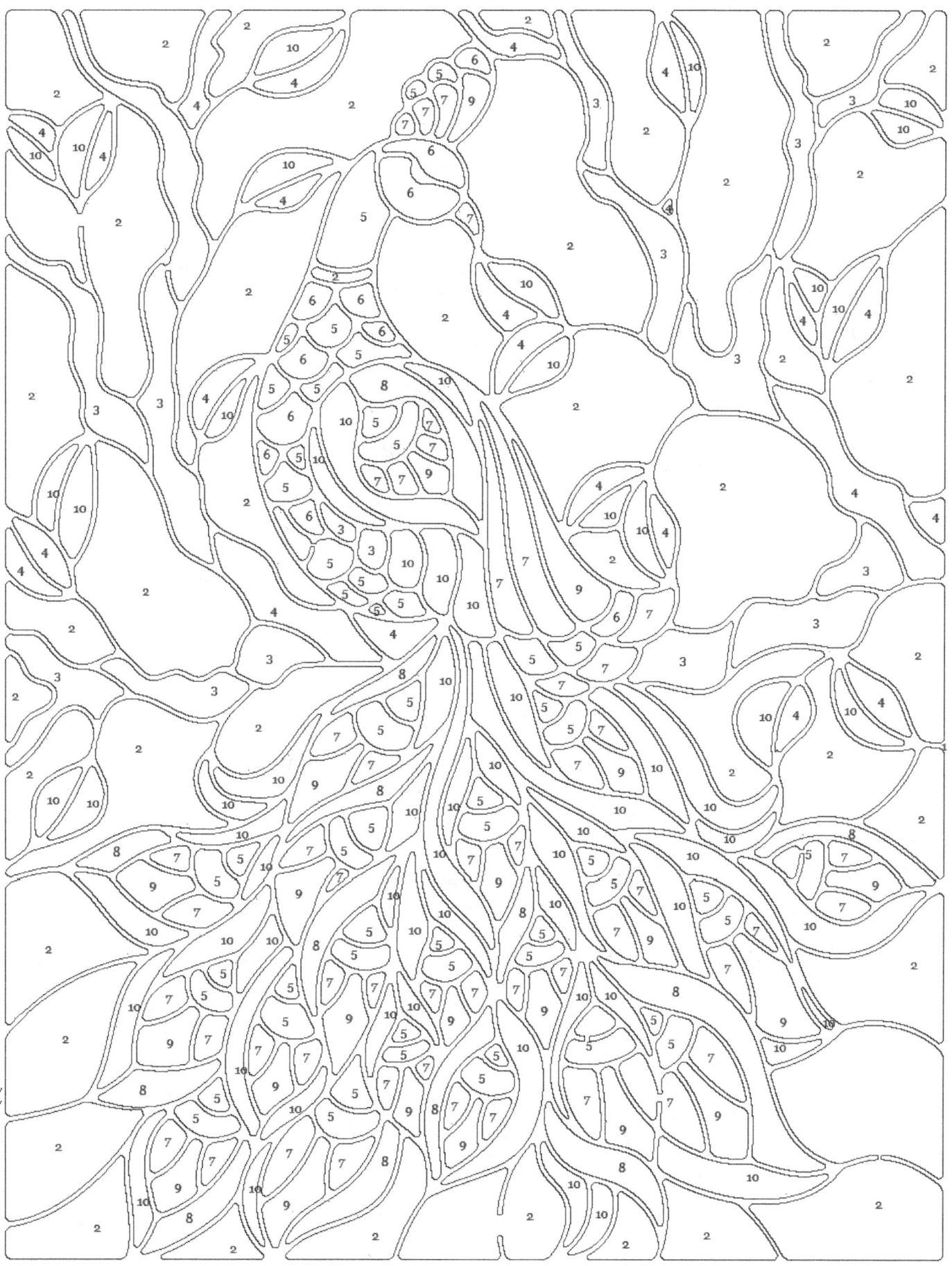

1. Black
2. Blue
3. Light Blue
4. Brown
5. Dark Red
6. Orange
7. Yellow
8. Purple
9. Pink
10. Gold
11. Green
12. Gold
13. Red
14. Dark Green

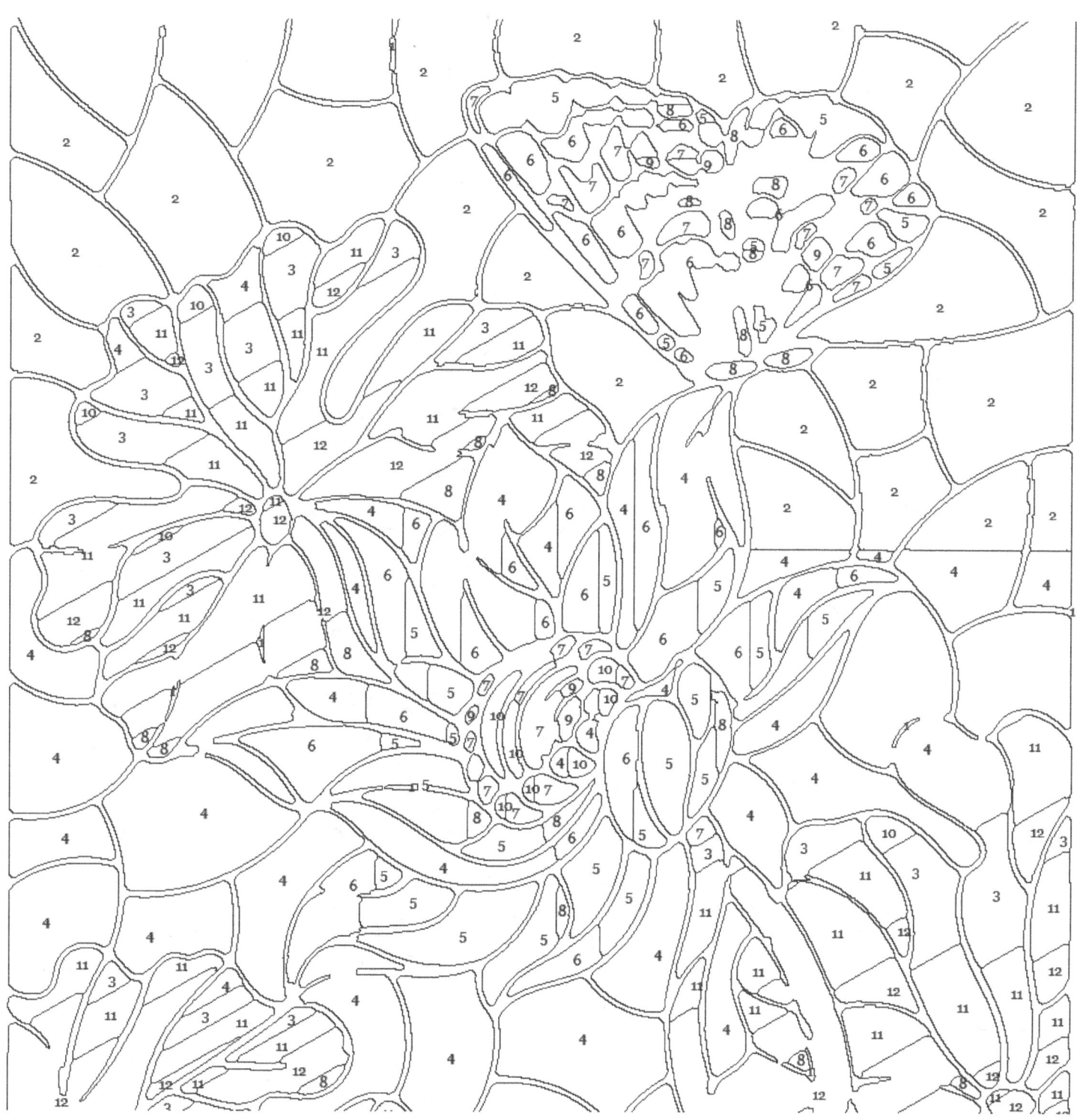

1. Black
2. Blue
3. Light Blue
4. Brown
5. Dark Red
6. Orange
7. Yellow
8. Purple
9. Pink
10. Gold
11. Green
12. Gold
13. Red
14. Dark Green

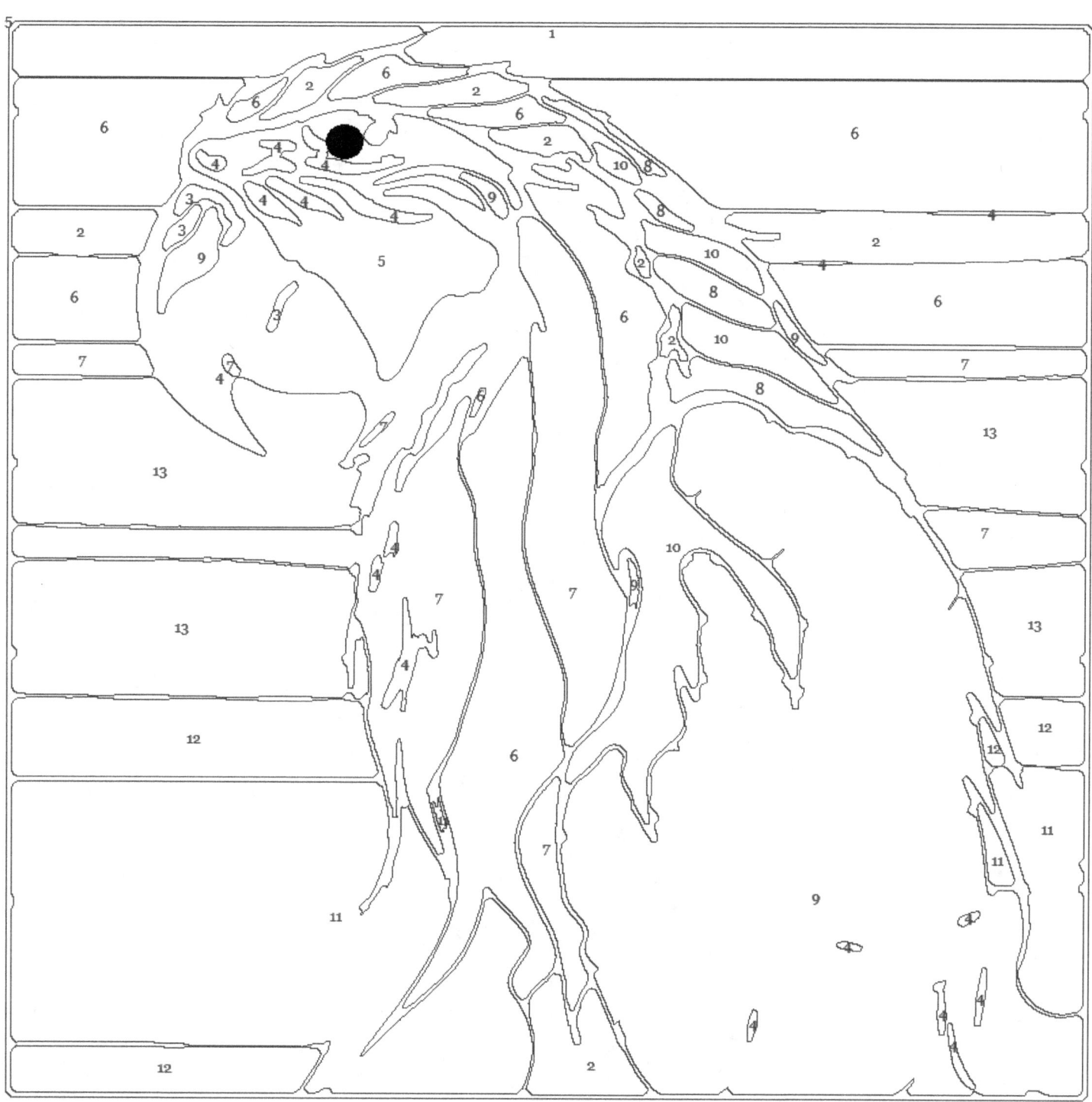

www.ingramcontent.com/pod-product-compliance
Lightning Source LLC
Chambersburg PA
CBHW080953220526
45465CB00008BA/3268